PAPER BIRD

PAPER BIRD

Robin Behn

TEXAS TECH UNIVERSITY PRESS

1988

Acknowledgments

Some of these poems first appeared (some in slightly different versions) in the following publications:

The American Poetry Review: "Geographies," "Living with Sister"
The Antioch Review: "Night Sail off Raber"
Benchmark: Anthology of Contemporary Poetry in Illinois: "Drownproofing Lesson," "Floating Gallery," "Last Bird," "Unopened"
Crazyhorse: "After Love"
Denver Quarterly: "Land's End," "Leavetaking in Winter"
Field: "Distinguished Flying Cross," "The First Angel"
5 a.m.: "Dear Sky"
Gambit: "The Angel in Sandusky" (from "Two Angel Poems"), "Two Waves"
The Georgia Review: "To Rise, So Suddenly"
The Indiana Review: "To the City of San Cristobal de las Casas"
The Iowa Review: "Paper Bird," "The Earth's a Little Lighter," "Recovery," "Letter via Stars"
Ironwood: "Over 102nd Street," "Whole-Body Count"
The Missouri Review: "The Drowned Among Us"
Poetry: "Four Years After Your Deliberate Drowning," "Angels," "Open Heart"
The Seattle Review: "Late Search"

For their support during the completion of this book I would like to thank Knox College for faculty research funds, and the Illinois Arts Council, a State agency with funding from the National Endowment for the Arts, for Individual Artist Grants. I am grateful to The MacDowell Colony, The Virginia Center for the Creative Arts, and The Ragdale Foundation, where some of these poems were written. And for years of friendship that fueled this writing, thanks to Deborah Digges.

Paper Bird, by Robin Behn, is published in cooperation with the Associated Writing Programs as the 1987 winner of the Edith Shiffert Prize in Poetry in the AWP Award Series.

ISBN: 0-89672-163-9 (paper)
ISBN: 0-89672-164-7 (cloth)
Library of Congress Catalog Card Number: 87-051682
Cover and section title page art copyright 1988 Jean Tuttle
Set in Baskerville, printed on 70 lb. Carnival vellum
Texas Tech University Press, Lubbock, Texas 79409-1037
Copyright 1988 Texas Tech University Press
Printed in the United States of America

In memory, D.G.

Contents

The Drowned Among Us

The blessed will not care what angle they are regarded from,
  Having nothing to hide.

Auden

WHOLE-BODY COUNT

Geographies

In Missouri in midwinter
I used to drive these 30-some miles in the dark,
cutting the headlights on the long, straight stretches.
As you, reader, maybe have held
someone you hated and loved in equal parts,
I'd hug the wheel hard in the vice of my
parenthetical arms
all the way to the Booneville bridge.

Nothing human
had crossed it for hours.
I'd saw the car back and forth across the silence
of the river whose name is the name of this whole country
till the balding tires on the metal grate
scared up such a shriek that whatever
anger had brought me this time
hardened in my chest, a black ball
slugged north, south, north across the water—

I'd let the Booneville city limits pass through me,
I'd smash my face through that wall of air
that says if we belong or not.

But my friend, while he lived,
loved this town right.
He didn't ever not belong.
Friday afternoons he crossed this bridge
and headed for the one hotel.
If you stare at the light-stricken
fins of these fish, then look up
to his window you'll see the white flag
of his shorts hooked on the ceiling fan,
the whoosking surrender
of a man who must be naked, who sits

very still, the slack flesh settling back
into the hull.

Even now, his ribs that always resembled
the riggings of fragile model boats
held by tiny glue dots, applied
with toothpicks in the shaking hands of nephews,
are giving up a little of their whiteness
to this landscape. The fish here
are whittled from a white like that
and likewise revise their quiet postures
when I reach for them.

I want this town to bless those who've come
with their small blessings, though their bodies
have stumbled through some fault in the light.
They are the geography I drive on, returning here,
out of the broadcast range of certain promises,
over the mica chips of their eyes.

Four Years After Your Deliberate Drowning

I still can't unimagine things.
Here, in the factual minutes before sleep

the daughter we wanted stands before me.
I know she is ashamed.

Why else would she appear like this, stoop-
shouldered, a string of beads in her hand?

"Our Father," she starts, and the chain jerks
through the pulley of her palm, down

into a well where the water
—being water—covers your face . . .

I think she would bail
all the water from the earth if that would make you

appear, once, *before*
I fall asleep, make you call off the dream

where we watch from the bleachers our daughter
tracing on the face of the pond her perfect

eights—those spyglasses, eternities.

Distinguished Flying Cross

Who thought then I would hold this in my hand?
Then, I had no hands.

Then, I was a thought, faceless, recurring,
some idea of home

that kept his plane from falling.
And everywhere below him

home appeared. Between him
and what he sighted—carriers, islands—

home was the throat that opened in the air
as the load dropped, *homing*, as he flew away.

Now I have found it, cross he never mentioned.
I've opened the box, let out the government smell.

Life line, line of happiness—runway in my palm
where a father wants to land.

Little plane in my hand, what are you the shadow of?
Viewed from what height, and how shall I get down?

After Love

Tonight, after love, our bodies so recently
returned to us, we lie apart awhile

and let the cold touch us
along the sudden boundaries of skin.

I can almost see above us where the air holds on
to some idea of us, the shape of our clear bodies—.

Once, two starlings got into my room.
From under my bed I saw them printing

their hard bodies in the shafts of sun
till the room was gorged with the image of those wings;

then there was only air
rasping air, my father's cleared throat, the black

birds knocked down.
This air

lies down on us. The weight
of my body lies down in me, lies down.

You slide an old song from its paper sleeve
and hold the black coin to the lamp.

And before it circles beneath the diamond needle
I can hear a few bars, playing

far off, where what's marred
seems beautiful—

Then our window takes on the open-eyed stare
of a musician playing wholly for herself,

testing notes off the walls
to find the shape of that body she's entered

in the dark. In that other
filled room

the birds are shoveled out,
the walls scrubbed clean of blood.

Here, the music heals the air. Tiny veins
beneath your lids finally turn their blue backs:

I see you scanning the private
constellations as you sleep, connecting lamp

to lamp as your one body moves up the lighted street,
getting itself home before you wake.

To the City of San Cristobal de las Casas

I'll give you back this light stashed three deep
in curbside tangerines

and this goldness someone loved in
more than once in this dead car;

and you can have the light, loose change
that clinks in words I don't know Spanish for

so I could say how, at dusk, the women
don their unsold goods

and make their way
through filigreed fields where thick

last thoughts of light pool
in the necks of stupid, beautiful sheep;

but first you must reclaim this
yellow bandage of light

—too much like what the amputee must see,
rising from the ether-dark;

it fell on the midriff of a young mother
who wanted my American money

and made her young son peel up her T-shirt, unzip
the inner panel of belt to produce

their last pesos (a thin, silver light
sweating on those faces), to trade

for my dollars so that they could cross
to the next darker country

(dark on the map, as if
into the cartographer's eye a cry

had welled up from some buried light
inside it, so that he colored it

purple—the first plum color of bruises
that marks where truth is still fresh in the body

before the blood comes
to cart itself away);

by daybreak those two will be far
from this city that is named for its houses

and farther, still, from somebody
—ex-husband, father—

who's hunting down their faces,
cloaked, as they are, in new names.

Angels

My father never said why—
not even to me, the silent one—

but silently, all through my childhood, he never
fixed anything

though the lathing drifted down
through the plaster ceiling

like the planks of a dock
we all lived beneath.

Meanwhile, he seasoned and stirred
his aquariums, his little wet houses;

like a god, he engineered tidal waves, resettlement,
even genetics—guppies' tails bred

into lavish, ripped flags of countries
our relatives never sent us letters from.

And the house went on with its own
sweet life. The roof turned algae-green, slugs

abided, my bedroom wall cracked
like a cup you slit your lip on.

—The pairs of fish called *angels*
had rubbery, nerveless lips

and killed each other for beauty
at night when he wasn't looking.

At breakfast I'd find it: a chunk
of silvery money with whiskers . . .

An angel is dead, I'd say.
And then, as if we were all already angels

and had a right to mourn,
a hush passed through the house:

the smaller fish looked smaller,
hours sucked by like snails,

dust filtered down and we opened
our gills to its mood for days, recircling our own

breathed air;
until finally

I took my allowance—the coins
they'd given me for some good cause—

and went out into the world for the white
paper carton with the wire handle

that grooved my palm as though a fish
with a cut lip were straining

for its life across my life-
line, and brought

the thing back
and set it down in front of him:

the silver, storebought wife
already married to the water.

Not East

I'm told that when they moved her
from the hall of the senile
to the hall of the dying, one
flight up, from 182 to 282
where she could keep the view
of the two girls walking home from Catholic school—

she swears they're my sister and me,
they pass on the far side
looking straight ahead like bloodhounds,
only now she can see the parts
of their hair like mailslots
moving off—my grandmother

asked the nurse to take her home.
She meant 182.
She meant, I suppose,
ground level and the wheeled cart
they let her use for passing out the mail
when she could still do that.

By now I guess she's riding in her half-sized nightgowns,
staring up at the flak-like acoustical tile.
I don't know. I don't look East.
East is Rockford, the world-traveled sky,
East is day draining down to stringy clouds.
Is them gathering

to storm, is the blueing
washed out of them into rivers that divide
the earth where it's already cracked and sore.
As, ascending, she'll see us in the blood maps
on the table where the doc
has closed her up and told us *why*.

Fogging the Bees

God, somehow I've made them drink
the gold from their bodies.
They drive as fast as they can
through the hot kitchen air—
they plunge into dishwater, cat's milk.
Those that have the strength
disappear into the hive,
come out staggering like gyroscopes,
one-winged.
Is loyalty like that?
I switch on the bulb.
The kitchen is a microscope:
between screen and glass, a smear of them,
a Rorschach, half
alive like my sister who claimed
she could decode that kind of truth
when she came home from the Buddhists,
dusted with peace.
In her head there was a clearing.
Names came to graze there, names
of perfect animals she chanted
till her head was a hive strung with words
for every kind of honey.
Now, the attic is a carpet of bees.
By spring they will be dust, the house
will inhale them, next winter gold heat
will rise through the blowers into the room
where my sister lies, larval.
I hope it is the right gold.
I hope that the *l* lodged in the word for it
will fall out when it stings her
and leave a god in the room to talk her
into her next incarnation: a life
both loyal *and* sisterly, like bees.

How My Mother Got Religion

Iowa River, 1948

In her mind the sticks
and curled shavings of the alphabet
shuffle like loose kindling
beneath her cursive curls as she crosses
the ice. The rich kids
she will try to teach to read
when she gets to the other side

are not part of the story, except
for what their mumblings
do to the alphabet—small minds lost
in expensive fur hats. Their brains

must have little stoppages, she thinks,
something like the clots the cardinals make
in the capillary branches
hanging over the ice.

One of them has a doctor father
who says he'll fix her nose
for a summerful of lessons.
A summer full of *cat sat fat mat rat . . .*

The ice is smooth
as dead champagne beneath her, and her nose,
like a goblet—soon to be more
like the stem of a goblet—
reddens with cold.

But she doesn't have to wait
for the August-long bandages

or the doctor who breaks her body
precisely where she asks;

the change will come this day
as she steps onto the bank and hears
the river let out such a groan behind her
that she knows God *so*
understands her wish for beauty
and all that will unravel from it
He's given it a human voice—

a cry so pitiful, so
unspellable, it rises from the river's depths
to drink down the ice and swallow
the frozen bridge back to her ugliness—
my mother, beautifully alive, one foot on shore.

Origin

Whatever it is that puts the dipper in my hand,
dangles me by the waist above my childhood,
I must close my eyes to see.
In the darkness my mother is turning to my father.
It is unusual. September.
I would like to have a son born in June,
she doesn't tell him.
Her diaphragm looks out from the drawer,
a cyclops eye. It thinks I
will be her intellect made flesh.
But I am born impaired, a run-on
sentence—slip of the tongue, his
on her—certain valves in me
won't close. *Negative attitude*
the kindergarten teacher says.
Already I look like a negative,
like someone poured my translucent head
full of salt.
The teacher has emergency instructions
she's to follow in case I . . .
None of this is known to me.
Later I will learn to read
and jimmy the files.
What I'm taught is I'm too bright
for any god to believe in,
and I must not, therefore, believe.
So childhood is a kingdom
but the kingdom lives inside you.
God didn't make it,
and here are its rules:
certain failed animals
are to be kept out in remote
parts of your body
you don't yet know you have.
Later, as a woman,

you'll discover the remains.
For now, each night, your mother
fills the gleaming socket of the spoon
with a fawn-colored medicine
and lowers it to you.
You see it descending—a wrench
to tighten the heads on the animals
too sick to go to school, to learn to spell
their simple, androgynous names.

Whole-Body Count

Tonight, love, the moon is cut loose from its stars.
If I knew what star-lit freeway it traveled,
what terrible beast in the camera-flash of dawn
it might wake and be the head of
(I might wake and be the head of).

I still have the album where everybody smiles.
Where my parents have forgotten the deaths
of their first loves, and my sister beams,
beautiful and theirs.
Beneath my pale face the dress hangs in folds
like the drape the photographer always hides in

or, long before you knew me,
the white sheet the doctors used to shield me
from their tiny lamp-lit expeditions,
their searches in my body
(the city there, the sunken stars . . .).

The body's made of chalk, of snow,
of something blind and perishing:

In all of the photos where I'm holding my left side
it is to cradle, to soothe
that fugitive
digging a small shelter in the snow.
I can still feel the blink of her heart below my heart—.

Above our bed this moon
can see you pull me from the watered dark.

Your solid, bouyant body
that would tow me toward the dawn.

How can I let you carry me to morning?
I could disappear halfway across.
I could drag you under
with the weight of my astonishment.

At St. Paul's

What I choose to remember
is the almost imperceptible
imprint of your ear
in the dune of my hip as you listened
for the tiny jig our cells made
in my darkness, so happy
not to be just an idea—.

That, and what I'm certain
the tall nun would have said to me
had I told her just now
I've done something for which
there is no metaphor,
no equal measure,
and the goddess of justice
with her two shining scales
stands slumped, one shoulder dropped
from bearing the weight of it,

as though a child
who'd promised to balance the seesaw
leapt up as I sat down
driving spine into brain,
and the onlookers ask
what makes a child so mean

though really they should ask
what mother has abandoned her,
and really I should answer
it was not to abandon her

I lay still as they sounded
the depth of my belly
where her new body hung
holding not quite still enough

for my light- and your dark-eyed
imaginations to see.

*   *   *

I had not thought
there could be a greater loneliness
than when you have emptied yourself
from my body—

In the whispering chamber that is shaped
like a cock and like a baby's head crowning
the lovers stand at opposite sides.
Like us, they seek themselves
in one another.
Like us, they appear
to maintain great distances—see,
they have their backs turned,
they roll each other's names
on their tongues like dice,
they confide them to the wall.

After they've gone
I press my body to the wall
where their names still orbit
as hers must spin among the dimmer stars
whose light comes such a long way
before we can name it.

But if we could refuse
to imagine that light,
if all of us refused
to see ourselves in it
and the things of our world—
chairs and dippers and horses to ride on,
things a child would love—
we would not remember learning

that some distant stars
die before we read them,
before we can conjure
what we'd most like to hold.

Letter via Stars

How hard it must have been for you—no roof,
   no body overhead—
how hard to learn to count by counting stars.

And how hard it will be when you outlive them all,
since they were born, and so have life-spans, star-

spans. So do the whirls born in different hemispheres—
one like sand, one like black earth—

who would have been your parents. I
am writing for us both, you know that.

I think that you are going to be a fine cartographer,
how else could we have found you in each other?

Last night, he taught me, your almost-father,
if I tie a string to Orion's right shoulder

and follow to its end in the steady wind that rises
when the stars put on their names and sweep forward
   to be counted,

I will see an eddy of snow, a faint balloon.
I think it is the galaxy

where certain children go
to live out their first lives;

it's full of smaller pinwheels and a sweet wind
to wheel them so the ones who have no lungs

can use instead the breath of the world—
the big world, the forgiving one.

Neon

I believe in the happenstance that saved me
as I believe in the wind that lifted your arm
to write the pronouncement of your fall.

Who thinks about it now? Maybe the tern does,
his ashen feathers like news sloughed off newsprint,
the shredded leaves of censored obits . . .

But no, that's memory, that's dangerous.
It was the summer we fell toward our deaths.
I notice, only now, we were trying to fall

out of love, which means falling
back into separate bodies
that are seawater, mostly.

I was teaching swimming at a 20-foot pool,
demonstrating dives from the deck.
Like a movie I walked backward to repeat myself,

fell back into the mouth of the concrete
trapdoor, felt my heart
flap up out of me, hover, refuse

a transplant back—.
I opened my eyes.
Saw a city of lights

in the sky where I was landing.
Then necklaces of lights
strung along the skinny footpath of a bridge

where a man sees his own face glint
in the windows of each passing car, a decal
that finally adheres, disappears

like the outline of my body
I stared up at from the lip of the 20-foot drop,
feeling, as I landed, what *ascension* must be:

yes, I "saw stars," but these were two red hot unison
taillights, and the car was the car sweeping high up
the river road, still wearing his face—.

When I came to, I came to believe
what I had seen: red glissando
defecting to the steadier, non-earthly stars. . . .

                  *   *   *

As a child what I collected was light.
I'd look out on the prairie
from the darkened Chrysler

to intersections, headlamps, shopping center parking lots,
streetlights lighting somebody home—
each buzzy filament contained

one day of future life.
My true love would be someone to collect them with
and neither of us could die.

—Sometimes I see us taking shifts
like the pilots who change guard,
waving across the air

as they keep the bomb aloft
and prevent their own returning
to a half-ravaged earth.

Ours would be a vigil of similar magnitude.
Were you coming to relieve me? To pick up the count
of lights seen from the water,

to give us more days of water to float in,
of each other's bodies,
and of those acts of love

which are a passing on of light, body
to body, two luminous batons
stretched out in the cattails, a neon

slip for a boat to steer home to,
or two rods of light crossed at their middles
so the plane knows where to let the loved ones disembark?

It was right before my fall.
You stood on the bridge.
Your shadow, the tern, hooked

its beak around the rail. I
was probably about to leave the water
—end of the day, the first graders gone—

as you walked off the tall building
of the air and met a surface
like tarmac. . . .

Now, when I am swimming and turn my head to breathe
it is you in my mouth.
Sometimes you are hard and young

and you want me to take you.
And sometimes it is now;
the questions I exhale to you so cloud the water

that your name, when I speak it,
sinks quickly from sight, its capital *D*
takes on the hideous, flat-iron visage

of the bottom-dwellers, more machines than fish,
their private flashlights in their foreheads saying
here's a way to manage the dark weight of the world.

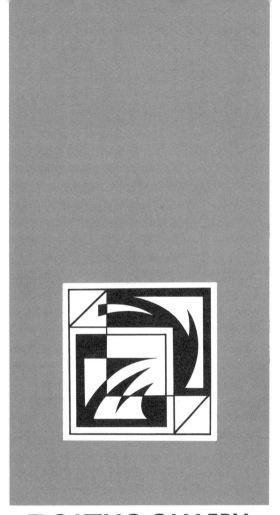

FLOATING GALLERY

Living with Sister

Up the road the stone-fenced lake;
all summer all I wanted
was to swim it—arm over arm
bring it in like blue rope.
In bed we felt it over us,

as though our mother had come in
to stand all night holding
a bowl of quiet water by our heads,
if we were thirsty or wished
to be born.

For Deborah, in Snow

No one knows at the airport hotel.
No one can tell me if your big and your small son
and you ever got there; whether the moving van—
a bird cruising just below the radar of bitterness,
its two frozen feet dangling down to score the snow—
left a track from here to there, unbroken.

I remember rescuing the three of you once
from the ruin of Detroit-built cars
on the yawning highway that maps
the boundaries of mutual custody—
We guessed through the dark, 10 m.p.h.
In front of us the wipers made gestures of ice

—white doctor's thumbs waved
before the blind eyes of the victim
when she briefly comes to—
and I thought, *Jesus, take me now.*
But in return, I want a sign. I want
this highway, forgotten under snow, and the hum

of its parentless, small bodies in ditches, this
not-quite-rising mantra—I want
this sound, this word made flesh in the trinity
of blankets you'll weave from my body
to warm them in the ditch until the white, spewing wings
of the tractor-angel come and lift them out at dawn . . .

But for now, just believe,
this ink can melt anything,
the dot above this *i* is a star you can follow,
and this voice will tow you to any waiting plane,
this sigh will be the contrail
whitely mourning your ascent.

In That Year

In that year when men's bodies still looked new to me,
each one a signed, original print with one
delicious flaw I might or might not recognize,
a young man—a boy, really,
only 21—gave me the kind of kiss
you ask yourself in the middle of
How can I move to the province
where this *is the mother tongue?*—
then drew back abruptly
and spoke in that bottled voice doctors
summon when their jobs require them
to say terrible things: *Do*
you know what a colostomy is?
and then became himself again
and answered his own question
by drawing my hand in his
all the way down his belly
to where the warm tape held the bag
in a kind of lasting kiss
on a kind of third mouth
and told me what feeling
he did and did not have there, and finished
by peeling my clothes off like bandages, slowly,
so slowly, it seemed he was thinking
I don't want to tear her body
still healing from the sight of me—
and then turned out the light
and taught me with the miraculous
remainder of his body
just where grace resides.

To Rise, So Suddenly

for Phil Mark

If it feels at all like going up in smoke—
the fire all around you so each sound you make
stokes it, each inhaling
burns you deeper—
then I think I came close once in a small church
in New London where we sang in black robes
to a packed house at noon:
you laid rungs in the air with your hands,
and we climbed up to an airy cathedral
that you led us into and into
till I felt the choir ring through me,
my weak torso swaying,
my small voice the clapper and
part of the bell . . .

Phil, the man who killed you was driving home
from your concert, still giddy
on brightness he felt from within. They say
his weak heart had stopped before;
he should have been resting, not out by himself
to hear his whole life filled
with forgiveness, measure by measure. His blood
started climbing high in his chest and his heart,
that *so* wanted this, shuddered
and closed on it. I
still want you to lift up your arms, to keep
the last chord sounding forté forever
though we're out of breath,
though time can't be sung back,
though a dead man who's driving is past being wrong,
though I am too late now to give you these words,
this grief, this disbelief, this vain applause.

Open Heart

Like the first black note
   that makes the key go minor
      the blackbird sags the phone wire

down to the fret called fear.
   So the dip in his voice
      is the bird's fault, I decide,

and nothing it hears in our long-distance talk
   makes its reptilian eyes turn inward
      though they do

turn inward like his voice, the hush
   a surgeon left behind in him
      last time in that room

where what blurs the *I* and *thou*
   is candied ether-air.
      Now, his voice blurs;

his body's canals
   are once again too trafficked—
      Gondolas, gondolas, nowhere to go . . .

Last time, he had a pole.
   Last time, when the soul assigned to him
      had fallen asleep in the boat

gazing up at white lab coats, thinking
   Cumulus, cumulus, nice day for drifting
      on out of this world,

he lay down the pole,
    just dropped it in the water.
        In exhaustion, I used to think.

When they fished it to the surface
    it stayed there,
        a long red scar,

as though the sun were always setting
    on the center of his body
        just above the timberline of fine red hairs.

The first time I touched there I thought
    Here is the pull-chain,
        and here is the light they screwed into his heart . . .

But I did not pull
    the way, now, the wire pulls
        at the distance between us

as if we were speaking
    through a tightrope of string
        between paper cups:

thimble-sized cup
    the nurse brings the pills in,
        thimble of water she metes out for the washing-down.

These are the dishes
    we're given in the afterlife
        when we have shrunk back to the size of dolls

to make room for one another.
    The scar, it seems, has risen
        to make room for another scar—

the phone wire resembles it, it
   transfers the vein of his voice to my ear.
      Meanwhile, the blackbird

listens with its black heart.
   It weights down the wire so one of us can clear
      that hurdle to the bluer air,

blood breath wings and all.

At Betty's

Far down the hill the expressionless bay,
and closer, someone hammering a house apart,
which I prefer. To look at the gray bay
I need some other thing in mind—
what cat under the water the triangle sails
are ears of, how many of them will drown,
and whether, later, I'll see an earless cat
and think again how pain, especially
the pain of others,
is a feat of imagination, of which
it is ashamed. Like thinking,
during the committee meeting,
when my friend's eyes went private
and turned toward some inner
spectacle of grief, that the axis
they turn on turns, on some other end,
the sudden spool of blood
unraveling from her husband's heart.
More likely, she is thinking
hard how best to cook a single fish
since he always did that.
But now I've decided
the eyes of the fish are hers, she's in
a warm, chance current. What I
ought to do now is bring her two fish and keep still
as we feed one each to our two bodies.
I can look at the bay if I think
the fish will come from there, that someone on the little
triangle has a net, that the net does not resemble
a branch of glistening nerves
as he hauls it up, too full.

This Poem

is for you whom the wind
neglects, whose pages
I found once, open
to a sun gone bright past kindness,
and there where all the color
had blushed white I lay my name.
Now, when I ask
and you pronounce it—
now, when, startled, you ask it
of the air—
my name flocks down again.
I can take your arm
in its sleeve of black silk, the formal
color of eloquence and endings and
the ruffles on small coffins
(selves before language:
selves before selves)
lowered into earth which is that
color, too, the color
silk the birth cord in my recent dreams
is tied with,
though which side of the tying
I'm on you'll have to tell me, love,
and whether you're there, too.

Floating Gallery

The room is white.
All the color is inside me, love.

But you can have a ticket
if you'll tell me, are there stars there?

Is the cold coin in my back
a skylight's winch?

Does my heart sound like thunder,
does it stuff you like the sun?

And the two points of pain where my long legs
like pilings hold up the makeshift

dock where you dock,
are they cold, like two nails

in a gun-metal hinge, a trap propped so long
that the animal whose head

was made to fit it exactly
has gone extinct with longing?

Or are they what I think they are, over my head,
two lit hands of a clock

that only marks seconds since that's
how pain passes, notch by notch;

two searchlights folded
like an oiled duck's wings, these legs

I let you divide like a heart to float up
on either side of you—a tired swimmer's carry

and you tell me to hold on—
but where

are you taking me?
Oh, my body, come back to me now.

The world has had enough of you.
I will wear you home.

Night Sail off Raber

Proximity should count for something.
A solid week of gulls
turning the sky, tightening
the blue lid on our small boat.
You lay on your back reading your books
and when the wind calmed you slept.
I saw my face float out, then,
but the water would not take it. . . .

You said it was possible to sail
by flashlight. At the bow
I fixed the beam on any leaf or oily feather
to set a course by. Anything
but you, your expertise.
A wind pawed the boat.
Below me the mast's shadow
broke across the backs of waves.
The rudder flapped from side to side to side
in your loose grip.
                    Seven days afloat.
To fall asleep by you again, untouched
in such a small, dry dark . . .

I saw them then: each ridged wave,
the cold hunched back of someone crossing under us,
gathering her wide shawl and running to the shore.

Land's End

Late-blooming bullet in his parting kiss—
I have carried the fever he gave me across the ocean.
It makes me see sad things.
Coming here, for instance, the train seats
divided by tables that limit
contact to accidental ankles,
chop us into head-and-shoulders portraits
like the kid across from me printed
on milk cartons: "Have You Seen This Child?"
Forwarded three times, his letter says
he finally left his wife, got followed
by a dog to his solo apartment
—inconsolable dog he stays home with now, alone.
It seems need is an illness things around him
catch. Here, I'm waiting for a sign
on the horizon: fleck of wreckage
from a ship that set sail before we met.
I'm waiting for the fever to break finally, formally,
out over these rocks.
Then, I'll back up, re-couple as freight cars do
to this last outpost of the world:
I'll put my face into the head-hole of the plywood pilgrim,
I'll pay a pound for a photo of my new, stoic body.

Leavetaking in Winter

I love the way we looked at the airport,
identical in height, your baggage
split between us as we walked to your plane.
I must have looked like I was going with you,
toward some happiness.
A few hours ago, I was
and so were you. Traveling
by kisses. Arriving and arriving.

Soon you'll see snow
banked in corners of the fields below
like envelopes I'll send you
without return address.
You'll recognize me there
the way you did when we first met.
You said we must have known each other
from another life—
                    Now I've come to see
it was a future life, prefigured
as this landscape I'm driving back into:

Dark gnaws at the farmhouses.
Inside, the ignorant lights have climbed upstairs
where they burn like smudgepots
through the snowy drapes of private rooms . . .

By now you must be landing
between two strips of light.
Someone else you love has come to pick you up, just

as I brake for a small thing in the road.
A bird. Frozen.
Its chest doubled, the song still inside—
Tell me what this means.
Not the song, but my stopping here
just as you reach home.

Unopened

I lasted all through yesterday—the hard day, Sunday,
the day the Lord sits head in His hands
gazing on the fuss He's made,

making us guess from the ink smell
and the slowly molding leather
of the hymnals what to do with ourselves—

it was a kind of test, not even looking
for your letter. I failed. I like too much
the way your letters come,

I think I bought this house to house them—
the private Mona-Lisa-smile-opening
of the mailslot, and inside, the miniature closet

where you'd think a shrunken nun was stowed but really
where your letters lean like sweat-stiffened dresses
someone's loved in standing up!

I looked. I found a nest.
Empty, in that box of dreams.
It is—where have you been?—the color

of your hair and shaped
like the whirlpool we fall into
in each other. Today

I found my name there—my name in your hand—
cast across a paper sky so white
it is the blindness of the falconer squinting

into high noon sun and telling
his bird to go there, and build a nest there,
and then he'll come.

Paper Bird

The way folding makes a weakness
in the paper, the way the weakness

lets the wings
move as if to fly,

the way, flying, he left me
and left behind this bird

as a token, I suppose, of how
we two

were a bird with four wings
that seemed to lift

our single body
a little off the ground;

so this bird
must remember when it was a letter

he could not quite write.
In the small hour when real birds

unfolded their cries
to test the air

for others of their kind,
hour when always before

he'd be waking me, his tongue
lassoing the hidden cry

buried in the throat
of our two-member species,

in that same hour he sat
at the old oak table

where first light ignited
the oval rings of wood into a pond-

mirage, and then from a height
the shadow of a parched bird

dove and broke
its body on the pond.

He saw, then, what to do.
How flight means resurrection.

And he wrote me,
by folding:

first, the patterned sheet
(as where I still lay, sleeping),

its white underbelly
too delicate to name;

then a paper plane
(each one-way passenger erased

by a snow of diamonds falling
from the ticket puncher's metal kiss);

then the plane's body
snapped to make a beak,

to make the beak point down at me
from his pillow as I woke. . . .

Bird, my name is robin.
All right. I'll un-evolve you.

Two blank sheets.
But what shall we become?

THE DROWNED
AMONG US

The Drowned Among Us

I know, since we can't find you,
you want only to be more with us,
not with me, only, but with us all
as water is, cool
beneath the shifting plates we
float on for a while.

We find the other ones
who've drowned: those who carried
in their lungs a last little pillow
of air, who always knew they'd come back
to lay their deep claim, round-
shouldered and smooth as if from weeks
bent in prayer, trying to save us.

But all you ever wanted
was to vanish into our midst.
I can see you that fall day
you stood on the bridge, ready, finally,
to be taken back.
All afternoon as I was turning
the brown garden I felt a wind small
as breath insisting
from the shore as you slowly, deliberately,
let it all
pass back out of you, anything
love had let seep in.

And now as long as water moves you will be
healed, and ours. At any shore
I can watch the water swathe you, rising

as it meets somewhere deep your naked form.
The day you left, your mother

filled a bowl with cool water, and brought it
to the boy who was feverish and waiting
for his brother to come back before he'd eat:
he puts his face in for what he thinks
must be forever.
And when he looks up
the fever floats in the bowl
where the water, like forgiveness,
burns with what is lost.

Quintet for Flute and Strings

For years I've been sad over somebody you didn't know,
somebody who walked the earth while you did—
but so what. Today you gave me a piece of music
you have written for the flute—the flute I learned to play
so long before the angel was given his assignment

to come down and uproot the garden of my heart—
and when I looked at it I saw how you'd plowed the staves' furrows
and unearthed the gleaming notes from the sky where it is blackest
(as, after someone's taken there they close the sky behind him
and keep it locked awhile until they know he sees

by the faint watts of his body and won't go grabbing
the stars from their sockets, filling up his pockets . . .);
when we played it I heard a voice as through a door ajar
that kept on not listening to anything it meant in me,
kept speaking in the soft voice I think God will use

to ask all the faces to lay down their tears
and wash the charred world
—and then everything sighed:
the chair first, offering its sturdy wood,
the four bowing arms it had rested on so long;

then the body, so amazed to be hearing that sound
that it rose from the chair where its life had been passing
and asked itself to dance, please, asked what
finally woke you, what woke you up so pretty,
what star gave you the money for such a silver gown?

Two Angels

The First Angel

In the picture he looks like anyone, fishing,
intent on the prospects of one pure line of thought
as though he's holding on to some great

kite that will lift him.
You had met him before at the docks once or twice,
a summer kid, you said, named Jim.

But how he happened to look for you that day,
lonely for talk, wandering around
where he thought you might live,

so that when you came out of your rented room,
heavy with news of your best friend dead
and the afternoon was gone and the evening

gone and the stars and the gutted street—
he was waiting there and took you,
he took you up in his small arms.

The Angel in Sandusky

At Baybridge a strip of land fastens this place
to the other side.
We'd walk the long causeway
across Lake Erie and back,
then on down the shore, tasting nothing.
What the wind delivers
we gathered up: bits of hair and glass, oars
rotting by the shore. Down here
the drunk's song still hangs
in the oak, a thin coat
covering the whole body of a tree a man
lay down under: he sang and woke whole
enough to walk.
And spring comes regardless of the song.
Because of it.

Eventually we
who were strangers lay down.
Most times at night.
With the dull weight of clock gears accustomed
to the hours we'd turn to each other,
and turn away, and turn.
And if we came close enough to be one body
it was his, and he rose from us new
as each hour, coming round again,
asking us to love.

Dear Sky

I've asked everyone,
but no one has as good a view
as you do over the comings and goings
and livings and dyings of us
here so small on this accidental planet.
I know, I should keep tabs.
Especially in light of the thick fog
the past is always slapping down among us
like deliberate roadblocks
to our obvious desires.
But I thought you might have seen her.
It strikes me this evening, as I see
you're having a fine old draw
from your expensive cigar—I can see
the dense smoke wafting up through the sunset
from the huge old lips of this Gertrude-
Stein-type guy lounging just
over the horizon where what looks
like mountains is his skirt
between his knees—
I thought maybe you could help,
maybe send up a signal
if you see her . . .

She's tall, for a woman.
She has a bald spot just above
her left ear that you notice when she's lying
on her right side, say,
on Sunday mornings when the light
comes in and warms it—
It's where her brother dared her

to touch her tongue to the spinning lathe
when she was fifteen and she only
got as far as her beautiful hair. I
was sixteen. By then she was older.
So many years older (two at least) that
kissing her was like going
to a very respectable party
where real adult things were being done,
and in the vacant parlor the sun
just sang with it, gushing
into corners that had somehow gotten dark:
the hinged collection box inside the piano bench,
even the slats of darkness
that forbade the piano strings from playing
unwritten, cacophonous songs—

       Dear sky,
I keep thinking I'll be walking through pines
and suddenly I'll see it:
a clearing just that soft, a spot
that shy, and I'll look to my left and where
her ear would be is all of her,
standing,
and the whole sky a patch like that,
sudden and touchable, and I'll ask her
in its presence to forgive me now
after so much troubled time.
And because there is no God
that looked down on her the night
she was beaten and her body was consumed
four times, though somehow
she rose and stumbled back in pieces
and into my arms;
and because nothing I could do

could repair her soul
though I flew at it with cloth
with glue with bandages kisses anything
and still there was a rift
between her and her body and therefore
between us
while the criminal crouched at some
boundary of our love,

I think now that passion
should be something like sunlight
while the sky looks on and nothing
in the process asks God to raise
the least hand to bless us.

Off Shore

That August he insisted he'd come to the shore
to watch me wade out to the anchored trawls
and convince one to ferry me across.
Whatever artful part of him wished to witness
this perspective—my body shrinking
like a pea shot from a cannon
where his love smoked vaguely orange and picturesque
as a scout fire—was the same part

that believed in the epic future
I must not have looked ready for as he consulted
binoculars: me, an occasional speck in the current
as I started swimming back across the Hudson.
Later, I realized, it was his presence
that kept the shore from getting closer—only more
to the left as the river pulled me south.
But maybe his presence, too, that made me lift my head

to see, mid-river, eye-level, straight toward me,
the brow of the barge plowing the horizon.
Believe me, in those minutes—days, I thought—
I knew I'd be swallowed down beneath the barge,
shucked out in its wake, sliced perfectly in two
so half of me would drift back to him
and half of me, to me . . .

But then the river captain,
a gray man in a gray cap,
more like a clothespin dipped
in river colors than a real live man,

saw what I was, and changed course.
It was as if an arrow aimed for my heart
had seen me
and decided on the air, instead. That's

when I knew I might make it across.
I pulled at the far shore, grinding
the water in the mill of my arms
till I stood, till in one gust
the oiled air hardened the cast of my body
and I waded out, finally, into the sting of my own weight
among the few things I still count on:
sky, shore, and where we stand between.

Recovery

After you left, I came
the long way home,
back to my name,
pulling my first body
like a sleigh weighed down
with just enough provisions
for a one-person winter, thinking
I should thank that woman
receding finally into the dusk,
retracting, for good,
her heart's delicate landing gear
to orbit the dark side of the brain,
this woman you loved
who I no longer was.
I knew then what we'd done
to summon her was wrong,
was a project our bodies
invented with kisses
as spendthrift as the smell
the earth casts off in rain . . .

Reply in Smoke

I set a match to the bird, that's all.
I hear a cry come out of it it

didn't know it had. Like ink

finding out it is black
and spilled—the vows

it is permanently laced into.

All the things you meant to tell me
lie down somewhere with what you said.

The climate is cold there:

the singed paper breast
and the water in the firebuckets

frozen to glass and magnifying everything.

But, because I'm generous in my love of birds
I am letting the wings fly back to childhood

—two verbs without a body—

all the way back to the chance-
toss of sperm, the brave patience of egg

though nothing will happen,

this time all there is
is space—the unseen smell

of smoke, the smell of paper ripe for burning.

Now, when I think of you—
the space between wings, a little smaller

than the heart that thought to make the wings—the wings

clap not
quite together as they fly

above the smoke's applause . . .

The Waders

Dry for twenty-five years in garages, they hung
by their heels in a kind of slow lynching
in which the victim—or his spirit—slowly drips
from the army-green husk that once conveyed his body
into the countries of striped bass
on blessed days in blessed Junes.
                                        Or so
I imagined my father's unmarried youth.
All I *saw*, though, were the waders which nobody spoke of,
which moved only when we moved
from one house to another where he rehung them
in the moth-eaten light of a new rafter.

My father was a *he*, whatever that meant,
but the waders were *they*,
as if the act of fishing
divorced him into two parts
he couldn't not maintain:

I think that the right leg
is the one he trusted
—right-legged, the way everyone in our family
is right-handed—
it's the leg he drove the car with
on respectable vacations to housekeeping cottages—

and the other, its opposite, isn't *left*
but rather *wrong*—
it's the leg that wants to eat us,
it's the other, sucking world, the one

that the right-legged world of wives and daughters
and dry paid-off mortgages doesn't prepare us for,

that one you must also take a step with
if you're my father,
one Sunday morning fly-casting all alone.

What you wanted was to take that foreign part of you
that will not go to church,
that believes not in "the Father"
but plagues itself with wondering

and cast and cast it out
onto the shiny foil surface
where the word for it is *prey.*

Meanwhile, you're thinking how solid
your chances are, the striped bass
—the very stripes of which prove
that this-world and that-world
can be beautifully, swimmingly,
united in some *other* beings
we might catch and eat—
are licking their hairy lips
just below the surface;

                    then
with a light/dark/light/dark *thwack*
one of them breaks the water's flushed skin,
erasing two-thirds of your green rubber body

which is when your left foot, your wrong foot steps
into the mudhole that sucks you way over
the tops of your waders. Each

next step puts you deeper into the cold and the cold
deadly world floods in—.

                        He says
it was like drowning and floating at the same time
(air pockets in the knees)—like being
both alive and dead . . .
I'm glad I'm alive he almost shouts, and changes topics.

(There was a branch overhead
for him to grab, my mother adds.
Her adjective is "lucky.")

So this is an elegy
for the waders, not my father.
This is their goodbye.

On the eve of his move
to the coastal retirement trailer,
soon to be garageless,
he's finally cut them down
and cast them out with the trash.

So goodbye to the feet that were always a little small.
Goodbye to suspenders that hitched them heart-high.
And goodbye, goodbye to legs
fat as the trunks of lucky trees.

Retiring, he's poised
on the lip of some stream that flows,
like all streams, in the one great direction.

The waders are delivered, too,
to their true resting place.
Soon they'll be smelly, burned rubber at the dump,

no different from the inner tubes,
dolls' faces, condoms—all

the rubber things we fashioned once
to try to ride away from life
or stare at a safer
version of ourselves, or stop ourselves
from happening—

But the waders are wiser.
Any foot can wear them, now.
The shoes sigh down into a pool
other waders can wade in.

Still, I'll always picture them—*him*—intact.
When he goes, against his will,
I think he'll go out floating
upside down into the other world,

body hollowed out, soul
filling with air as he rises, feet first, drawn back
by the doctoring grip of deliverance, the schools
of bass he dreamed of catching
slapping him back into a world

which isn't *other* anymore,
where he can put his head under
the water's great gray skin,
all safe and unperplexed
like it was in his first darkness.

The Earth's a Little Lighter

Florence Behn, 1895-1984

what shall we do
with the ashes says my father

what shall we do with the part of her
that mattered   that unburnable

mother-thing the air won't swallow back
what if it's the soul

or is the soul the space
of air she once displaced

It's for him to decide
—but—

what if we brushed her
over him   lovingly

he'd look like he's standing in the rain that rains
just after the end of the world

If she were my mother
I'd want to add a little water

offer her small planet
back to the sky

and I'd want the stars to know her
as she went on her way

Over 102nd Street

It is late. All the small things I believe
have curled upon themselves, and from a window
higher up than mine a woman sails
gray leaves of ash onto the downdraft
between buildings
that carries this street down to the river.
Mornings, I go down to the river
where I first saw her,
as if a boat might float in and she'd be on it.
She was walking by the pier,
naked beneath her raincoat, her pockets
stuffed with syllables of bread.
And I remember thinking, before I knew anything,
that I could touch her. It seemed nothing
fell away from her, or everything,
like the rain, like the wheel of pigeons rising
from the rope of bread falling upward as she spoke,
and I wanted to say to her—though stories
of the flesh wear thin with too much telling,
and close, finally, a parenthesis, like the two
black wisps of hair along her cheeks—
I wanted to say one thing
so pure, so white, it puts a hole in the air
and I'd pass through to where she is,
kneel by her cloth shoes, open my mouth for bread,
and keep coming back until she knew me.
But now to even
walk down
to her station by the pier would take longer
than all the years since I first saw her.
As I cast her image out

onto this late, cold breeze,
this is what I see:
We will be crossing in a stairwell, one of us
ascending, wings opening
in our throats, and words will spiral down
wet and gray across the city like the ash
they have to rub into a dead woman's eyes
to keep her from telling what she's seen—.
But it is late.
And I was thinking only
of all the women I have loved
across great distance and great silence, without regret.

Late Search

All day on the radio flat static
filled the car as I took
the river road, deep
into Vermont. I knew you only
by the glint on the water, reflected
off some deeper, moving thing like clean
white bones, or fish.
Vermont, late fall, the sun
backing off a bit each day—it seemed a good
place to find you, heading north
into the dark.
        I found an inn
by the river and lay all night, the wheels
still in my head and the river
and the river road stretching on like
your breath into my body, but still

I could not dream you.
I saw only the vacant waves, opening
and slamming shut, slamming shut some
floating door. And then from nowhere
your palm, cool
on my forehead, closing softly
like the last word.
Then I didn't know
which side we were on—the water calm,
too close to see or else too far—
as if you'd wakened me
from my dream, into yours.

Birch Island

Everything here flew here, walked
on February ice, or was loved enough—
like the cast-iron bedframe—
someone hauled it in a boat.
So, loon, who loves you
that you arrive at the dock,
your one broken rudder of a wing
drifting, your head
dipped down in gray nectar? I'm
out of breath, wondering
if you are. Let's both go back
to being stones on the south shore.

Last Bird

By the time I found you
your feathers had flown off

your heart that had already beat
more times than mine

had gone to live in the chamber
of perfectly still numbers

Only the gunnels were left
—the boat that rowed your song through air—

and this sharp place
between my shoulder blades

from the beak
where you entered my body

Everything that's lived
lives on in some other thing

you in me
I'd like to think

Once I knew a man
who kissed everyone goodbye

everyone   everyone
though we didn't see it

then he went to kiss
forever the bottom of rivers

So the body he entered
passes through us all

as you set sail in me, bird,
we set sail in him

I write this on a clean wind
I sign our name to it—robin—

Two Waves

When they ask, tell them
I followed you.
It's simple.
They'll believe it.
Say I sat on the great
chair of water, rocking,
waiting for your return.

When you came you said don't
touch me, so I lay down instead
in a basin of light—
wedge of sun
that hounds each wave—
and side by side
we kept the watch, the space
across which life repeats.

And now since nothing has changed
we must be moving. See,
the drag of black water on our bodies,
yours, then mine, and behind us
our skins. All that's left

is *rise* and *pitch.*
Is *motion, echo, light.* This
is what we wanted, isn't it?
Outdistancing these bodies,
isn't it?

Drownproofing Lesson

Hour upon hour I keep them hanging there like jellyfish

under the vast umbrella of air
until they re-open the primordial eye
that sees just light and dark

the way searchlights on their bodies,
all night afloat, would show alabaster clams
moored in black glass.

But no one will come tonight with lights, snorkels, hooks.

This is the lesson
in how to let go of the overturned boat
as it sinks below you

even if a plumb line
that starts with your spine
seems tethered to the hull—maybe

your mother and father are on board,

maybe the icy minnows of their fingers
can't quite buckle
the fat orange life vests, maybe

your sister is screaming below you
but all you can hear are the halos
the O's make, breaking the surface—

Here is what you'll do:

you won't think of the safety flares
in bundles marked "emergency"
inside the hold. You will only

watch the blind eye of the water
as it watches you, and feel on your back
the prickly gaze of indifferent stars.

This, then, is why we bow our heads,

and let the cheap bauble of our bodies
dangle
in the face of terror

like a whore so casual
the murderer loses interest
and goes back into the street—

If we manage, it's called *grace*.

It's why God planted two
hollow wings in our lungs
to let us hover between worlds

if only we can train ourselves
to master the postures
of the bouyant dead.

That's who we must look like

in the ever-longer intervals
between stolen breaths
so that a boat that's already

set out from some shore
will spot the islands of our backs
crowning, like births.

Notes

"Geographies" is in memory of Tom McAfee.

"Drownproofing Lesson": *drownproofing* is the term used in Red Cross Water Safety Manuals for teaching people to survive for long periods in the water by hanging, effortlessly, in a dead-man's float position, raising the head occasionally to breathe.